C[illegible]y Aesthetic Interiors

by Lady Henrietta Jones-Hunter

The allure of 'old money' INTERIORS

The allure of 'old money' is not hard to understand. It's not just money, it's money they've had for a long time, 'old money', don't you know!
Any fool can get lucky, win the lottery or make some money here and there. Keeping the money in the family, passing it on and creating generational wealth, that is another story altogether. There is something comforting and yes - reassuring about old money. It implies stability, comfort and even wisdom.

Old money interiors are all about comfort. There is no need to show off because the money has been there for a long time and everyone is used to it. The 'nouveau riche' may still have a need for validation, (at least until they become old money themselves. That is if they don't loose the money altogether.. More common than one might think.)

While the middle classes may be a bit embarrassed about money and the new money is usually rather keen to show theirs, old money is comfortable with their status. Naturally, even 'old money' would have been 'new' at some point, but with every passing generation, the family becomes more refined and more comfortable with the notion of money. Old money doesn't throw money around, but doesn't think about it all the time either. No penny pinching and no crazy spending - they are somewhere in the the middle of the golden mean. They would be wouldn't they?

Comfort and refinement are the key concepts reflected in the old money aesthetic interior. Everything is supremely comfortable and, oh so - refined. They've had enough time to discover the most comfortable furniture, plus they've had the comfortable furniture for a long time. Sometimes generations. They had the money to buy the best sofa and they've invested in, perhaps, reupholstering it, rather than throwing it away and starting anew. It's not that they've never made decorating mistakes. It's just that they only kept the good stuff - their decorating mistakes are long gone by now.

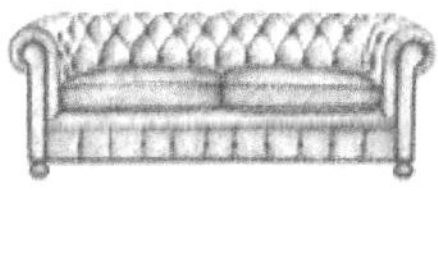

Chapter 1
Classic Architectural Elements

Let's start with bigger picture. People with old money often live in old houses. Well - old mansions one should say, (sometimes palaces). The longer they've had money, the older the houses. Georgian architectural gems, grand Victorian villas or perhaps art deco townhouses.
These architectural styles though very different usually share certain 'old money' characteristics.

High ceilings:

Who doesn't like high ceilings, preferably beautifully ornate ones? Impossible to heat properly, yes perhaps a tat impractical, but desirable nonetheless. Intricate mouldings, a little bit of gilding (or in the case of victorian style rather a lot of gilding). Sometimes these places, have been the old money seat or family homes for generations. High ceilings usually come with other architectural features like panelling and high skirting boards. Modern skirting boards are a poor imitation of 'old money' style. If you've seen a room where the skirting board is over 25 cm high that's old money design style of you.

Grand staircases:

Think glamorous movies: the staircase in "Gone with the wind" or one of those found in an 18th century French chateau - stone build with beautiful ironwork. They don't make them like that anymore. (That's why we have lifts!) A grand staircase is a work of art in itself - though it used to be a practical necessity. Grander houses would have had several staircases: The main staircase being grand, (exquisitely designed low steps and carpeted with deep pile rugs) to be used by the family and a secondary lesser (usually wooden) staircase for the servants to tip-toe around and do their jobs.

Marble fireplaces:

Most old houses include fireplaces in the principal rooms, but only the crème de la crème have marble ones. The 'old money aesthetic' interior is very likely to have a beautiful marble fireplace, intact. (Not a plastic one, installed later) The fireplace itself may not be the main means of heating the space any more. There is most definitely central heating - after all fireplaces are a very inefficient way to heat a room. Old money usually had the good sense NOT to rip off their beautiful fireplaces - they are still there adding finesse to their grand interiors. People who restore old houses are generally on the look out for the right fireplace to fit the proportion of the room - not an easy task and is its going to cost, yes you guessed it, rather a lot of money.

Large, floor to ceiling windows:

Large sash windows, French doors, perhaps even with pretty, decorative balconies are another feature of old money architecture. Natural light, fresh air, sometimes magnificent views are some of the perks. Few things can improve quality of life more than plentiful natural light. Graceful windows are a staple characteristic in authentic old money interiors - and very difficult to imitate. If you have them, enjoy and thank your lucky stars. If not - fret not, I have included a cheat sheet with tips for you, later on.

Solid original floors:

It is said that you can always tell a lady (or a gentleman) by the shoes. (Of course these days it is mostly trainers, but still.) - One can also tell authentic old money interior by the floor. Yes - look down, check out the floor. Solid wood or marble - in keeping with the architecture of the house. They may be covered with an old Turkish carpet, or a French Aubusson, yet we can still catch a glimpse of the old floor peeking at the edge. Old wooden floors mellow with time. A solid wood floor, would be needing regular upkeep, polishing and repairs,

Extravagant floral arrangement, mirroring the chintz upholstery, beautifully bathed in soft light.

definitely high maintenance, but longer lasting and more refined than alternatives. Marble floors are great for warmer climates - even so - best used sparingly to avoid the nouveau riche look.

Well proportioned Rooms:

Old money's old houses would have large airy rooms and usually a lot of them. A library to house the family's extensive book collection? Yes! A drawing room or sometimes two, morning room (a space that catches the early morning sun). Of course! Dining room, Breakfast room, conservatory, smoking room, (*though naturally nobody smokes any more, 'old money' are au courant, on latest health advice.*) small parlour, front parlour, ladies parlour, -you get the idea. Spare bedrooms and of course staff quarters.

Naturally, in a house like that, many changes would take place over the years to suit each generation. Perhaps a bedroom transformed into an extra bathroom, butlers pantry turning into a modern laundry room. The old TV room disappeared and at some point a yoga studio appeared, somewhere near the stables or by the pool. The successful Old money family is usually adaptable and makes smart health conscious decisions.

above: marble fireplace, luscious floral arrangement, chesterfield sofa.
left: period staircase detail, typical regency.

Ralph Lauren interiors photographed in London c2024. Oversized sofas, marble fireplaces, stacks of books, flowers...everything is timeless.

Chapter 2
Timeless Furniture Styles

What sort of furniture is very 'old money aesthetic'? You'd think Chippendale, Queen Anne, Georgian, and Louis XVI right? The best of everything right? Well, not quite!

Though of course it's possible that the old money family may posses a few pieces of the above - they generally go for comfort. It's their house, they live in it, it is not a museum. Over the years anything uncomfortable has been removed. Either sold off to Christies, or is in the attic under layers of dust and cobwebs.

There is a well-stuffed sofa (often two identical chesterfield sofas), for comfortable get togethers. Something to put your feet up, FT in one hand, drink in another. Upholstery is maybe leather, silk (always slightly worn silk rather than brand new) damask or slip covered in something washable, for the dogs you know. Elisabeth the late Queen of England had slip covered sofas, for heavens sake, so why not? The dogs, the cats and the children (future generation of old money!) use it with abandon.

Generously sized armchairs, oversized plump cushions made with remnants of the best quality hand printed fabrics, mixed with hand embroidered pieces and inexpensive modern finds from Amazon. Comfort and fitness people, comfort and finesse.

There are several lamps scattered everywhere casting their warm glow on little side tables. Now, those little side tables may be chippendale, Queen Anne tor IKEA- it depends. There are fresh flowers of course (never faux) and real potted plants. Scented geraniums tend to do well in those vast, high-ceilinged, under heated rooms. Abundance of photographs, some in black & white and maybe even the token ancestral portrait.

There is an exquisite Georgian-secretary desk with a drop-front writing surface, a secret compartments and ample little pigeonholes housing the long defunct crested stationary, (everyone e-mails these days, or texts.) Still, keep the stationary just in case.

Bureau (or secrétaire as the French like to call them) are easy wins. A few years ago you could pick them up really cheap because they were unsuitable for the bulky 1990's computer. Nowadays of course computers are light, sleek and easy to use with an elegant little French secrétaire. The old money had the foresight to hang on to theirs (or brought down the old one from the attic storage). If you still have one - dust it off now - lets start using those noble old mahogany pieces.
Beautiful walnut secrétaire examples are often seen incorporated into a modern home office for the old money aesthetic. Add a modern minimalist desk chair (Le Corbusier if there is one?) and a sleek latest apple airMac and we are in business. A sophisticated

workspace that combines beauty, classic elegance with the latest functionality.
So it's all refined mish-mash - nothing really matches but everything coordinates. The truth is this sort of interior took several hundred years to come together- you just can't rush it. Second hand shops, auctions or Ralph Lauren is the closest example I can think of, to achieve this sort of aesthetic. Or hiring an established interior designer like Colefax - they have the experience to do the mix, really well. Naturally, that kind of interior solution, will no longer be actual old money - it will now simply be quite a lot of present day money.

Bedrooms in the old money style, may be furnished with large half tester beds, or grand four posters or just simple , comfortable divans. The mattress though will be good quality, possibly the newest thing in the house. Old money are not stupid, they do value a refreshing, nights sleep. Bedlinen is usually rather plain, white and always 100% linen, hemp or cotton. Never silk though, which old money views as a decadent, unsustainable new money idea, generally laughed at, in old money circles. A bit naff really. No silk and certainly no 'faux' silk, ie polyester.

Bedside tables may be antique and rather valuable ones at that, perhaps even a set of Queen Anne chest of drawers in mellow walnut. Or they may be ornate, hand painted chinoiserie, solid mahogany or just good, old pine with some vintage bedside lamps.

The truth is old money interiors are layered - they will contain items from a good mix of styles, some older than others. New or old they are all sharing the common denominator: that of being supremely comfortable and fairly robust. Occasionally items are hideously ugly, but thats old money for you: They do not care what you may think about their interiors.

Old money furniture was built to last, can be used without fear. Withstood generations and witnessed rowdy parties, arguments and fisty fights. Sure they may be marks on the grand dining room table, scratches on the sideboard... oh my god is that a real bullet hole? Well these are the furniture with a story to tell. Probably quite a few stories.

above: a formal dinner table is set awaiting guests, with bottle of wine, classic chandelier, and abundance of red roses. left: reading lamp, comfortable armchair, bookcase- staple interior trick. Its an invitation to enjoy life - Sit down with a good book & enjoy!

Detail of curtain & upholstery. Note that the curtains are lined in stripped ticking fabric - attention to detail is everything!

Chapter 3
Rich Colour, Luxurious Fabrics refined Textures.

What is the colour of (old) money? Old money and old textiles go hand in hand. Vintage silk Fortuny? Yes! Grandmas ancient patchwork quilt - reworked as a bedstead. Of course!. Hand printed Bennison fabrics, maybe, Colefax & Fowler chinz, or Jean Monro perhaps? Antique French and Belgian linens, sumptuous Indian silk saris, hand embroidered with gold thread. All these can happily co-exist.They never look outdated and the high quality means they last and last and last. The dogs may have left them a little worse for wear, but they still look glorious in their frayed beauty.

Investing in high quality items means they practically never need to be replaced. Old curtains reinvent themselves as new cushions, quality old upholstery gets patched up - of course new things are added too, if needed. Re upholstering an old sofa with new fabric is never cheap, but it does literally reincarnate the piece, breathing new life onto an old interior.

Natural fabrics may get moth eaten sadly - but they still age gracefully. They do require regular cleaning, hoovering and airing - but that's what gives them the distinct 'old money' feel.

Magazines will often show immaculate rooms in shades of white and cream- these interiors most definitely need money to create and maintain - but they are most likely very new money. The old money aesthetic is almost always defined by including, at the very least several - old, well-used things. Sophisticated schemes that evoke the ambiance of old money homes have colours usually mellowed with time or intentionally chosen to look soft. Nothing too stark, jewel tones sometimes present - but no harsh primary shades. Chalky gentle blues, faded fawn, biscuit, soft rose, chartreuse greens, butter yellows, mahogany browns...All in indeterminate shades, so they whisper rather than shout beauty, comfort and ease.

Typical old money aesthetic fabric:
-Fortuny silk (exquisitely rare - but you can pick up scraps for a small fortune at 1stDibs... I mean I wouldn't, but many people do)
-Silk velvet (preferably not too moth eaten)
-Grandmas ancient patchwork quilt/crochet (old money loves old family...but not too cottage-core.)
-Bennison fabrics (not really old-old money because they are mostly from 1990's but the look & quality is there.)
-Colefax & Fowler (country house staple -)
-Jean Monro (as above but more exclusive, you need to buy through a professional decorator)

A restrained interior with calm colours: double chesterfields set in front of the marble fireplace. A lacquer tray is ready with tea & fondant fancies.

Chapter 4
The Art, the Antiques & the Heirlooms

Old money interiors are a mixed bag of authentic antiques, family heirlooms, classical sculptures (mostly raided by a great great uncle from Greece in the 1820's!) as well as more recent children's drawings and polo trophies. Most of the time the fine china (Spode) never gets used or is in the attic collecting dust. Nonetheless if you are going for the look, buying an antique china set is an easy win. These fell out of favour with the invention of the dishwasher (live-in housekeepers don't wash dishes any more). There are stories about the late queen Elisabeth (as old money as they come) and Lady Margaret Thatcher (daughter of a grocer, definitely not old money, but first female British Prime Minister. It counts for something no?) - both ladies allegedly enjoyed donning a pair of marigolds and doing the washing up. I am sure it can be very relaxing as an occasional pastime, but not as a regular housekeeping chore. Old china sets can usually be bought inexpensively in English auction sales and they look fabulous all stacked up in a china cabinet. Though of course one needs the space for a pretty china cabinet.

Silverware are particularly difficult to live with as they require constant polishing to stay gleaming and tarnish free. Polishing silverware is not only time consuming and laborious - it's also rather toxic -so we'd give it a miss. The old money interior would have one or two gleaming candlesticks though, perhaps silver, perhaps brass. Little souvenir from the good old days.

Art collecting is very much an old money pastime, many art collectors are seriously old money. Works of art, exquisitely framed send a clear 'old money' message. One can always tell people with money by a quick glance in their home interior: because they have real, actual paintings on their walls. Framed! Old money started buying their art before the artist found his/hers way to the hall of fame, so prices were still reasonable, you understand. (Even Picasso had to start somewhere.) Then each generation just kept adding more paintings, more sculptures, extra figurines and sports trophies, they each have their story. The more the merrier. The older the family money, the saucier the stories to tell.

Within 'old money' circles, it's not uncommon to have one of the salons or principal bedrooms covered with hand painted chinoiserie wallpaper, in silk. These are often found in the grandest English mansions and often painstakingly restored...Or perhaps best: avoiding the urge to over restore and allowed just to be, in their faded glory. If you don't have an art collection yet, but aspire to the layered old money aesthetic, a chinoiserie room is not a bad start. It gives a rich, colourful lived in visual foundation - though by no means inexpensive. De Gourney in London offers fine, bespoke examples, in stunning colours - all at a price.

above: 'earlham' design by DeGourney London. Hand painted chinoiserie is of course an extravagance, but the colours are simply divine. right: another beautiful panel hand painted on silk.

Soft colours, natural fabrics and botanical themes... marble fireplace & plants. Note the rather plain, mahogany bureau in the corner.

Beautiful, hand painted cushions are works of art in themselves. Too good to sit on?

Chapter 5
Plants, cushions, frames & other tell-tale details,

This is the sort of detail that's hard to fake, but reasonably easy, to buy into. Old money interiors include REAL plants, never fake. If you are the sort of person that kills everything, I have tips for you in the next chapter. Old money interiors is usually awash with potted geraniums, (rare varieties please), scented hyacinth bulbs, and other green plants, year round. New money people may have a regular florist or gardeners, but old money will most likely have green thumbs and thriving indoor plants. Don't ask me why - it is one of life's mysterics. It could bc that the good energy of the plants attracts the money - or the money buys the plants, we have the classic chicken and egg scenario.

Antique or vintage frames in gold or silver leaf, are usually present in most rooms, and an abundance of feather filled cushions. Sagging sofas can be made supremely comfortable with the addition of extra down filled pads and a cosy throw blanket. (Not too many throw blankets, as it can look messy and trying too hard, which is not very old money.) Cushions are also used outdoors in the garden, the veranda and even in the kitchen. Comfort is everything - those things are there to serve.

Which brings us to the next thing. The bed is not the place for extra cushions. Pillows YES! Cushions NO! Having to remove an assortment of cushions before getting into bed, is not particularly comfortable. Pillows with washable linen covers are much more like it, a bit of lace at most but usually plain and easy to launder.

Art in beautiful frames may be present in every room, even in the kitchen and the bathroom, though not watercolours of course... Frames are sometimes so god damn fine - they are worth more than the art itself. Old money doesn't believe in skimping on framing. There is usually at least one old mirror in every room sometimes with original gilt frame. Glass may look a bit mottled, if it is real vintage mercury or silver leaf glass - it often does. This gives everything a softness which can look very flattering indeed. Sometimes we do see old frames with new shiny glass - mirrors do break and occasionally have to be replaced. Heartbreaking I know...but life goes on. What breaks can be replaced with something of equally good quality. New art acquisitions are sometimes framed reusing older frames - yes it can work rather well.

Antique or vintage frames may be present in every room, even in the kitchen. New frames can be expensive, but 'old money' doesn't believe in skimping when it comes to framing.

above: Bennison Fabrics based on the original 18th and 19th Century designs. Fabric lamp from fermoie

right: collect plenty of samples before we start. Its a good way to hone your taste and clarify the interior vision. Planning and scheming ahead.

Creating 'old money' elegance in your home

THE CHEAT SHEET

All very easy of course, should you have the grand, classic architectural elements mentioned earlier. You know, the impossibly high ceilings, the oversized windows and the marble fireplaces. Not everyone has an old house and even 'old money' has to buy a new house or apartment now and then. Therefore we have created a cheat sheet with sassy tips, clever contacts and creativity.

Don't fight the architecture.

Well, first of all - don't fight the architecture. I repeat: **don't fight the architecture**. Best not to attempt adding intricate cornicing and period details on a new build - the proportions will most likely look wrong and it will all end in tears. It is however sometimes possible to add a vintage fireplace from a reclamation yard and install hardwood floors. This is expensive and not really practical, unless you are refurbishing or renovating a place, but it is possible.

The good furniture layout

It is usually wiser and more economical to start with a good furniture layout and let the architecture be. Including just one really good antique piece in a sea of IKEA can elevate the interior to 'old money' status. An old queen Ann chair can be reupholstered in a modern fabric, with a couple of matching throw cushions to tie it all in, with the removable (and supremely practical & washable) IKEA sofa cover. A couple of vintage candlesticks to add atmosphere - and real beeswax candles. Expensive but they smell divine and purify the air - what more could you ask? Depending on the size of the room, try to include at least one really comfortable place to sit, adjacent with a small side table to rest your china tea cup and the philosophy book (ok maybe the iPad) you are currently reading. A reading lamp close by, is an excellent addition. Never rely on overhead lighting - especially headache inducing fluorescent lights!

If you like to have friends round to entertain - then you need at least two chairs (or a small sofa plus chair(s).) Real china for tea/coffee cups, quality glassware and a pretty vintage plate - will make anything taste better. 'Old money style' right there - not on the latest Nespresso machine, which will be out of vogue in a few years time.

Simple furniture arrangement - it feels both intimate and luxurious. Somewhere comfortable to sit, somewhere to put your drink and something attractive to look at. Small spaces with poor natural light - can still manage to look inviting with side lamps and gathered fabric lampshades.
The photograph was taken in 2023 in a retail environment it is based on Coco Chanels private salon!

Grand four poster statement bed.
Designed by Soanes Britain www.soane.co.uk

In the bedroom

In the bedroom stay away from the all matching everything - but do buy a decent mattress, just like 'old money' does. Saggy, old mattresses are not 'old money' - they are a health hazard to be removed ASAP. Nonetheless, do bear in mind that in recent years, the cost of a decent mattress has sky rocketed. Resist the need to go bankrupt buying one. Even the best mattress will need replacing after 7-8 years, therefore budget accordingly. There is no mattress in the world that will actually cure backpain, for that you will need regular yoga and maybe some top notch physio. Therefore buy something good to sleep on, yet be realistic about what a mattress can, and cannot do. Outrageously expensive mattresses are not 'old money' they are just 'thrown' money.

If you live somewhere with cooler winters, an old-fashioned eiderdown (they can be commissioned new here https://www.thedormyhouse.com/products/eiderdowns
Or here: https://dearestviolet.com/) with a fabric of your choice is a lovely touch of tradition, comfort and that 'old money' feel. Especially in Jean Monro fabric - but almost any floral will do. UK based readers can buy hugely discounted remnants from here: hainescollection.co.uk

'lit à la duchesse'

Sketch for 'lit à la duchesse' often referred to as a half tester bed. The canopy may be fixed on the ceiling or on the wall above the bed. The custom of receiving visitors while reposing in a large and elegantly fitted out bed was practiced in France during the eighteenth century mostly by aristocratic women. - hence the name 'duchess style bed.' Traditional four poster beds, usually require high ceilings, but a simplified canopy can become a glamorous addition to rooms with more average proportions.

otherwise known as a *'half-tester'*

Another option for the aristocratic 'lit à la duchesse'.
These days mostly found in museums, modern interpretations can be both practical and attractive. Reimagined using washable fabrics rather than the traditional silk, can also provide valuable hidden storage underneath the high bed. The canopy helps with acoustics and diffuses light contributing to a calming space. Who knew that such a sumptuous addition to a modern bedroom, can also become a practical choice..

Nightstands (and most bedroom furniture) can be hand-me-downs (hand-me-downs are very 'old money', you save money, therefore you have money.) Often they come from the inexpensive local junk shop, eBay or auction site. Even if they are hideous, it doesn't matter, as long as they are clean, woodworm free and solid. Just add matching lamps for a touch of symmetry and soft glow bulbs (something warm around 40w). It goes without saying any lamps/electric items bought second hand will need to be rewired/checked out by qualified electrician. It is a hassle, but it has to be done.

Money spend on beautiful lampshades (sometimes gifted people can make their own, I salute you.) will always elevate the space. Opaque paper lampshades can throw hard shadows, whilst translucent ones lined in gold or rose fabric will offer the most flattering light.

If you have the space, adding decent storage in the form of an old armoire, a vintage tall boy or a chest of drawers in old mahogany. Definitely not all three though, unless you want your bedroom to resemble the local junk shop, pick just the one. I must confess to a weakness for a modern, immaculate clean, chest of drawers from IKEA. Not as good looking as queen Ann walnut- but the drawers do glide with ease - so very important for our mental health, during those chaotic mornings rushing around, trying to find matching socks and get dressed.

Thoughtful details on bedside tables elevate daily life providing comfort and finesse.

Bedroom inspiration for 'old money aesthetic'. Restrained colours, soft rose, chalky blues and mellow green. Natural fabrics please!The 'corona' style bed above by OKA (sadly now discontinued) can be achieved by a good curtain maker.

Unleash your inner gardener.

Perhaps the easiest tip for 'Old Money vibes interior, is also the least expensive one too. Yes, yes, yes, to unleashing your inner gardener.

Old money interiors include REAL plants, never fake. What if you live in a dark city flat, where nothing grows though? Or perhaps, you are the sort of person that simply kills everything green just by looking at them? Easy solution: just buy inexpensive potted plants from the local supermarket and decant into a very pretty and unique vintage cache pot. One with little claw feet, preferably. (Yes you have to hunt them down, but they are out there.) Every 3-4 weeks, bury the plant with dignity and replace. Potted geraniums, rare varieties, hyacinth bulbs, green plants are year round staples. You will feel better too, surrounded with all those plants exuding good energy, fresh air and 'old money' vibes, so win win.

I include a list of flowering bulbs you can force indoors (and some relatively cheap plants) for each month of the year. Some will last a lot longer than a month but do not keep past their best. If you have outside space or a green house they may be resurrected, but in a small flat best to recycle and replace. Do check what is locally available and keep the display fresh and well looked after.

Peony season is to be celebrated.

It is short but glorious!

January: Cyclamen

February: Hyacinths

March: Azaleas

April: Orchids

May: African Violets

June: Begonias

July: Peace Lilies

August: Gerbera Daisies

September: Kalanchoe

October: Chrysanthemums

November: Christmas Cactus

December: Amaryllis

Well thought out details are simple: fresh cut flowers, vintage mirrors, a sumptuous cushion...

cut flowers

In a small space and a tight budget, choose either a live plant OR cut flowers, you may not need both. It is lovely though to include cut flowers in plentiful supply - sometimes these look best if you cut the stems really short and use an old container for that unmistakable 'old money' feel...

A nice touch is to include a tiny posy by the bedside table or the kitchen counter top. Remember to refresh the water or at least top it up every couple of days or so.

Old money trick to prolong the life of your bouquet: It is said that adding an old penny in the water will help them last longer. My own preference is to add a drop of bleach/sprite. (Just a drop, as we'd rather not overpower the flower scent with the smell of bleach).

January: Carnations

February: Daffodils

March: Irises

April: Tulips

May: Peonies

June: Roses

July: Sunflowers

August: Lavender

September: Dahlias

October: Chrysanthemums

November: Poinsettias

December: Holly branches

Seasonal bouquet providing ever changing interest.

A small bud vase is perfect if you only have a few flowers. Using a pretty glass tumbler or even an ornate teacup, can look exquisitely nonchalant!

Changing your fresh flowers with the season will
ensure an on-going visual feast.
It can also make for a relaxing, very 'old money'
pastime.. Flower 'arrangements' don't always have to
be elaborate or expensive, sometimes a few daisies
are the epitome of 'old money' chic.

12 golden rules for the 'old money' interior

1. No more white walls. Paint your room a colour, no sorry! I've been told beige is not actually a colour. There are other neutrals, https://www.paintandpaperlibrary.com
2. Embrace 'brown' furniture. Practical, inexpensive, and robust. Looks best combined with fresh upholstery and (real) green plants.
3. Create layered interiors with stacks of books, mismatched lamps, and vintage look textiles. A little bit of clutter can be good actually, but do avoid over-furnishing. Keep pathways clear.
4. Wooden floors, always popular, preferably look into reclamation yards for sustainable, older floorboards.
5. Choose vintage rugs like Persian, Turkish, or Aubusson—second-hand is good and nothing has to match. Layering over sisal or wooden floorboards.
6. Maintain consistency in materials for curtains and chair coverings to create unity. Larger rooms can take oversized patterns. In a small room you could use the same fabric for curtains and chair-coverings to create solid foundational

unity, an impression of spaciousness. Then it really doesn't matter how many different things you add on top, or what colour carpet you use for that matter.

7. Plush curtains can disguise ugly windows, by keeping the colour tonal with the walls. Placing the curtain rod closer to the ceiling creates the illusion of taller, more elegant shapes.

8. Bedrooms are private spaces - but should retain some element of grandeur. A canopied bed can be achieved with a curtain rod and some ingenuity. Avoid trendy, oversized bedsteads - they are unlikely to stand the test of time.

9. Ideally there is a fireplace—preferably marble or stone, definitely not plastic.

10. Professionally framed art on the wall, it shows respect for the artist and exudes refinement.

11. Real plants, real flowers... need I say more?

12. Add something really contemporary - new tech, a modern light or art. It's not a time warp!

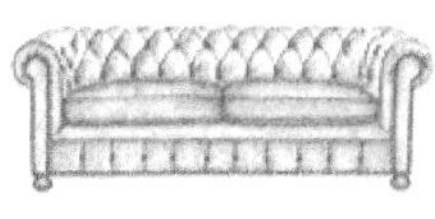

A messy room is just an opportunity to create! Take your own before/after photos. Clean, declutter and create layered interiors with stacks of books, mismatched lamps, and vintage look textiles -

top: inspiration can be found in all kinds of places. The interiors in the 'succession' or those of 'Bridgerton' can be a fun starting point. above: colourful throws - preferably washable can alter the colour palette.

Quality Fabric remnants sourced from eBay or specialists like https://hainescollection.co.uk/collections/fabrics. Opting for oversized square pillows (65x65cm) in crumbled washed linen, rather than 'dry clean only' throw pillows...

Top: Slow decorating is very 'old money'. Take your time when it comes to choosing paint colours. Start by painting samples directly on the wall and look at them under different light at different times of day. Let your thoughts settle before making any grand decisions. Bearing in mind colour will look different depending on what other colour you put next to it.

Left: colour charts are merely a starting point - don't solely rely on them when choosing the colour palette.

Tips for really tiny rooms & rentals

Creating Timeless Elegance in Modern Homes: Practical tips on how to achieve the old money aesthetic in new homes, including tiny, city rentals.

Make the walls, the sofa and curtains the same colour. It doesn't have to be exact, but keeping it tonal or in the same colour family. For example choose different shades of blue, or various shades of green with small touches of pink or primrose yellow.

Generally use only one type of pattern and keep it quite small. Stripes are a good example, Gingham, (also called Vichy check) or tiny scale abstract prints.

Create strategies for blending vintage and modern elements seamlessly. For example by keeping the colour consistent, you are able to mix furniture from different eras, without any worries.

Small rooms generally look better with deeper, richer colours (avoid white, which can look stark).

Unfortunately, many rentals come pre-painted in ugly, stark white. If the landlord refuses permission to repaint: Embrace it! Adding crisp white window treatments, washable white linen cushions, and oversize mirrors in vintage burnished gold frames. Switching to soft glow lightbulbs will work magic. Especially if you invest in side lamps or sconces.

Mixing vintage and modern elements can create a timeless look. Here the fireplace is original to the room c1830, the mirror is French Louis Philippe, late 1800''s and the chairs contemporary copies of 1960's models, with new upholstery.

Some furniture companies will allow you to order 'on approval' giving you the opportunity to try furniture in situ. You may still have to pay for delivery/collection, but preferable to being stuck living with mistakes.

above & below: large, gilt framed mirrors are an easy win. So is purchasing furniture 'on approval,' tags still on.

Hunt down large, gold framed mirrors and lean against the wall - they will double both the light and the space. Be mindful to check exactly what they reflect though, a common mistake, often overlooked

Use lucite furniture in moderation. (one or two pieces at most). - they don't age well, can be a trip hazard...such a nuisance really!

Generally avoid having anything plastic on show, including storage containers. Choose wooden chests instead, which can double up as table tops or seats by the addition of a plump cushion on top.

Disguising wiring whenever possible and think carefully before bringing any item in your space. It needs to be beautiful, as well as essential.

Use larger, not smaller furniture, but less of it. A lot less. Make do with a dining table that doubles up as a desk or a bed side table that is also the dresser...

Interiors from Netflix series 'succession' include all the classic 'old money' elements. Florals, sculptures, lamps art, candles...the usual suspects.

Include one (real) plant or vase of fresh flowers, otherwise keep surfaces clean.

Your interior should include one super large basket with atractive blankets/cushions. It becomes invaluable when it comes to hiding clutter for emergencies. Cover clutter within basket using a blanket. Don't forget to subsequently remove clutter - especially if it consists of old pizza cartons. Definitely NOT 'old money' aesthetic .

Make detailed lists to avoid impulse buys. Instead buy with view to longevity and value. Buy pieces that you'd love to take with when you move to a bigger/ better place. Allow your interiors taste to get more refined, taking time to enjoy the process.

Choosing wisely & knowing what to leave out

As already discussed 'old money' interiors are all about comfort. There is no need to show off because the money has been there for a long time and everyone is used to it, by now. Therefore there are certain things, old money simply never buys, or needs for that matter.

Anything over branded with prominent logos. For example: Yes, to discrete branding in Howard sofas - solid investment bro, but those Hermes cashmere blankets with huge H pattern? Not so much...

Fast Fashion interiors. Its a thing now, would you believe it. Oliver Bonas-esque ceramics, fiddly frilly things trending on Instagram, faux this and faux that. Buy now, throw away in three months time.

"Faux" plants, flowers or lawn. Its a big NO, never mind if they look *so* realistic. They emit harmful toxins and chemicals - who wants that?

More than two 'decorative cushions' (as opposed to pillows) on the bed. They just get dusty, get in the way, providing next to no comfort in return.

Random accessories and 'decorative' items, (with no story behind them) simply cluttering up the space.

Buying expensive matching furniture 'sets' - everything from the same shop. Expensive and not very old money chic. If you already have a matching set though - don't waste it! See if you can break it up, by using the various pieces in different rooms.

Huge 'show' kitchens, with granite tops, overpriced appliances and fancy gadgets. Too many people buy kitchens for their imaginary lifestyle. How much cooking do you really enjoy doing?

A grant library room furnished with suspicious uniformity - 'Books by the yard' for people who never actually read. Technically we should have already read & loved at least 80% of the books we display. Otherwise donate the books & use the space for something else.

Art they don't actually like. No need to pretend. Display old magazine covers you enjoyed or photos of the kids. Anything but pretentious art.

Televisions in every room. I mean really - do we need to spend more time looking at our screens?

*Allowing interiors to evolve,
taking your time and enjoying
the process.*

Epilogue: Embracing Timeless Elegance

Congratulations on starting your journey to create an 'old money' aesthetic in your interiors! Worth remembering that this style is about more than just appearances—it's a philosophy of longevity, value, and the joy of evolution.

Each piece you select should be chosen with an eye toward its enduring quality and potential to appreciate over time.

Our furniture and decor should tell our own story, choosing pieces that will stand the test of time and will continue to do so for generations to come. Yes to that beautifully crafted antique desk or to (the slightly overpriced) Persian rug, these items are not just purchases; they are investments in our home's future.
Allowing interiors to evolve naturally. The 'old money' aesthetic is never static; it adapts and grows, just as families do.

As we acquire new pieces, let them blend seamlessly with the old, creating our very own tapestry of history and personal narrative. Mixing styles and eras—but also letting go of items that no longer work for us. Thats what auctions are for!

Eclecticism is at the heart of true 'old money' charm, that and enjoying the process of curating our space. This is not a race, but a leisurely stroll through the world of interior design. Take pleasure in the hunt for the perfect piece, relish the stories behind your heirlooms, and find joy in the gradual transformation of your home into a sanctuary of timeless elegance.

In essence, the 'old money' aesthetic is about cultivating a home that exudes comfort, refinement, and a deep sense of history. Making thoughtful choices, cherishing quality over quantity, and creating a space that feels effortlessly elegant and uniquely yours.

> “Smart choices, cherishing quality over quantity, and creating a space that feels effortlessly elegant and uniquely ours”

Thank you for reading this little guide! If you enjoyed it and would like to stay in touch and read more on the subject, do get on my mailing list:
henrietta.j.hunter@mac.com

Forthcoming books in the series to pre-order now:

"old money" aesthetic wardrobe:

how to exude that old money style, fashion & finesse

"old money" aesthetic entertaining

how to be the gracious 'old money style' host

Author: Henrietta Jones -Hunter
Publisher: Luminous Publications
Imprint: The 'Gallery
ISBN: 978-0-9571233-2-8
henrietta.j.hunter@me.com

My notes

Thank you for reading!

Stay in touch - looking forward to hear from you
henrietta.j.hunter@mac.com

Thank you for reading!

hope you enjoyed it.

Printed in Great Britain
by Amazon

57964769R00046